THE CHRISTIAN MUSICIAN

PIANO · VOCAL · GUITAR

Classic
Praise & Worship

ISBN 0-634-05485-6

HAL•LEONARD®
CORPORATION
7777 W. BLUEMOUND RD. P.O. BOX 13819 MILWAUKEE, WI 53213

Visit Hal Leonard Online at
www.halleonard.com

Contents

AS THE DEER

Words and Music by
MARTIN NYSTROM

As the deer pant - eth
You're my friend and You
I want You more than

for the wa - ter, so my soul long - eth af - ter
are my broth - er, e - ven though _____ You are a
gold or sil - ver; on - ly You _____ can sat - is -

Thee.
King.
fy.

You a - lone are my heart's de - sire _____ and I
I love You more than an - y oth - er, so much
You a - lone are the real joy giv - er and the

AWESOME IN THIS PLACE

Words and Music by
DAVID BILLINGTON

BLESS HIS HOLY NAME

Words and Music by
ANDRAÉ CROUCH

BLESSED BE THE LORD GOD ALMIGHTY

Words and Music by
BOB FITTS

CELEBRATE JESUS

Words and Music by
GARY OLIVER

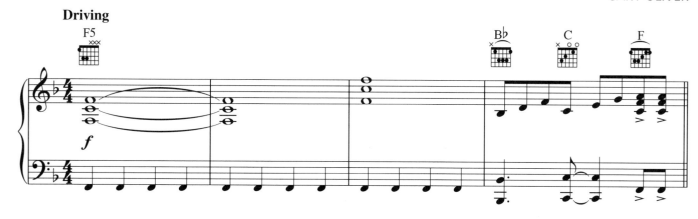

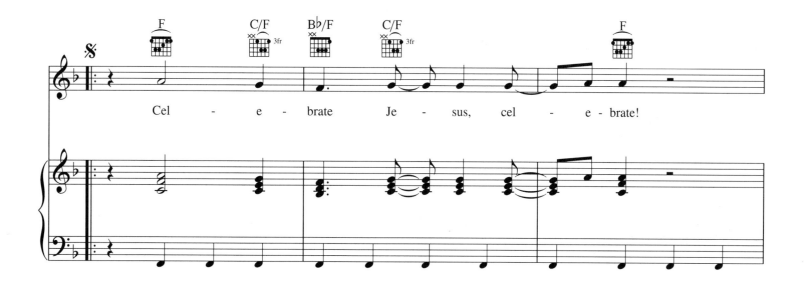

Cel - e - brate Je - sus, cel - e - brate!

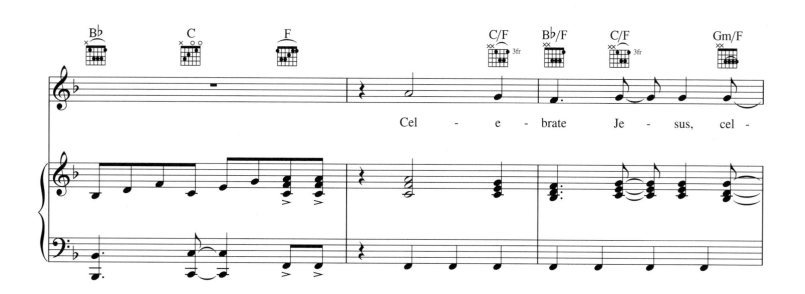

Cel - e - brate Je - sus, cel -

CHANGE MY HEART OH GOD

Words and Music by
EDDIE ESPINOSA

CREATE IN ME A CLEAN HEART

Words and Music by
KEITH GREEN

GIVE THANKS

Words and Music by
HENRY SMITH

GLORIFY THY NAME

Words and Music by
DONNA ADKINS

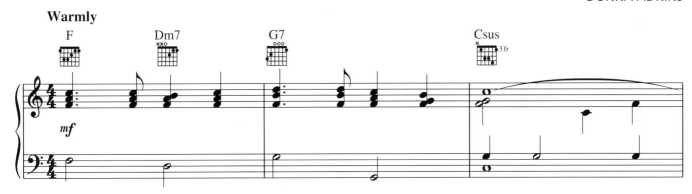

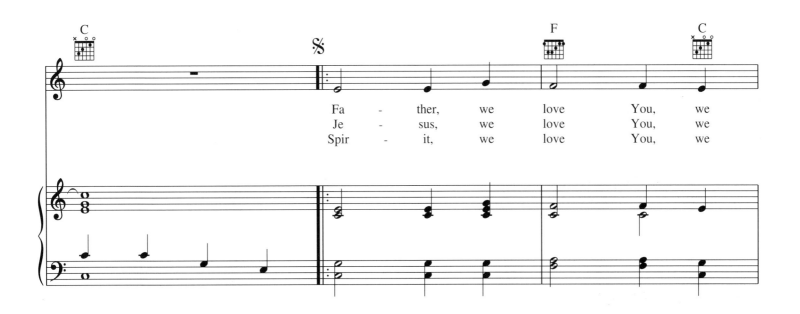

Fa - ther, we love You, we
Je - sus, we love You, we
Spir - it, we love You, we

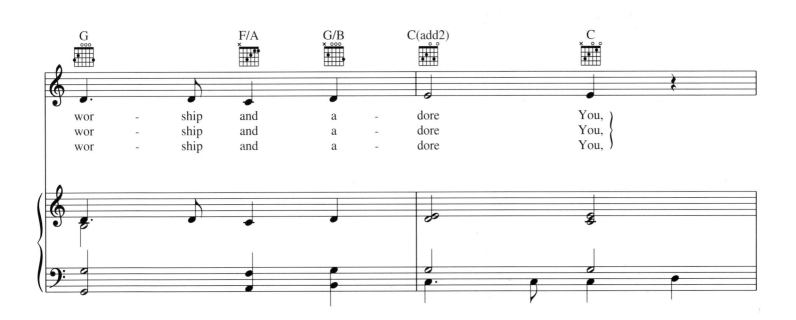

wor - ship and a - dore You,
wor - ship and a - dore You,
wor - ship and a - dore You,

GREAT IS THE LORD

Words and Music by MICHAEL W. SMITH
and DEBORAH D. SMITH

HE IS EXALTED

Words and Music by
TWILA PARIS

HOLY GROUND

Words and Music by
GERON DAVIS

HOW MAJESTIC IS YOUR NAME

Words and Music by
MICHAEL W. SMITH

Lord, _ our Lord, _ how ma - jes - tic is Your name _ in all _____ the _____

I EXALT THEE

Words and Music by
PETE SANCHEZ, JR.

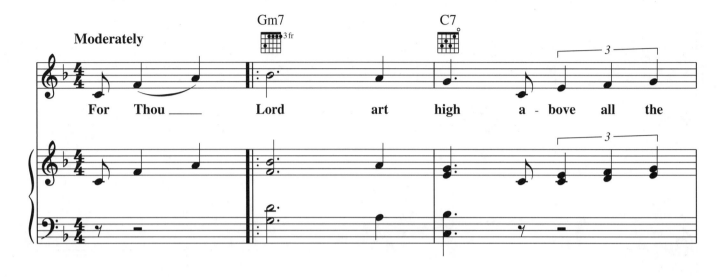

For Thou _____ Lord art high a - bove all the

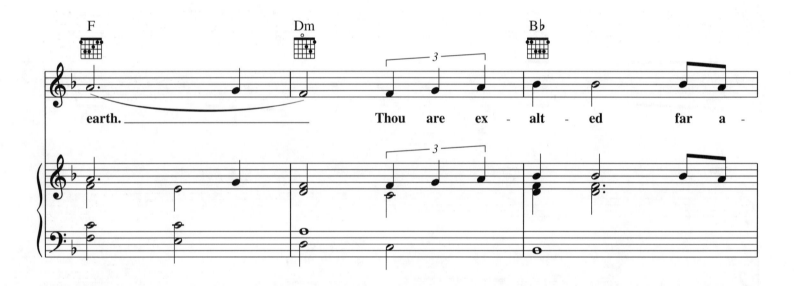

earth. _____ Thou are ex - alt - ed far a -

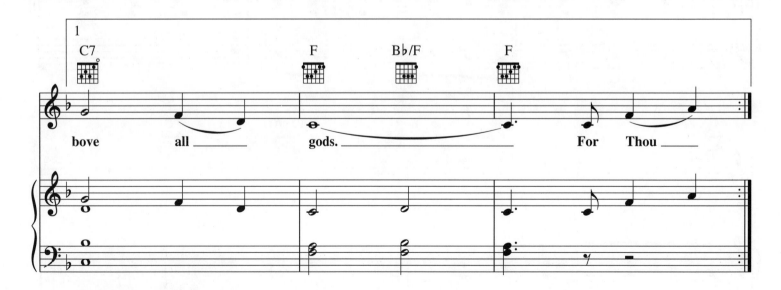

bove all _____ gods. _____ For Thou _____

I LOVE YOU LORD

Words and Music by
LAURIE KLEIN

I SING PRAISES

Words and Music by
TERRY MacALMON

I WORSHIP YOU, ALMIGHTY GOD

Words and Music by
SONDRA CORBETT-WOOD

JESUS, LORD TO ME

Words and Music by GREG NELSON
and GARY McSPADDEN

JESUS, NAME ABOVE ALL NAMES

Words and Music by
NAIDA HEARN

LORD, I LIFT YOUR NAME ON HIGH

Words and Music by
RICK FOUNDS

LAMB OF GOD

Words and Music by
TWILA PARIS

MAJESTY

Words and Music by
JACK W. HAYFORD

62

MY LIFE IS IN YOU, LORD

Words and Music by
DANIEL GARDNER

MIGHTY IS OUR GOD

Words and Music by EUGENE GRECO,
GERRIT GUSTAFSON and DON MOEN

MORE LOVE, MORE POWER

Words and Music by
JUDE DEL HIERRO

MORE PRECIOUS THAN SILVER

Words and Music by
LYNN DeSHAZO

NOW UNTO HIM

Words by DAVID W. MORRIS, Based on Jude 24-25
Music by DAVID W. MORRIS

Lyrics:
Now un-to Him who is a-ble to keep you from fall-ing, and to make you stand in His pres-ence blame-less and with great joy,

OH LORD, YOU'RE BEAUTIFUL

Words and Music by
KEITH GREEN

OUR GOD REIGNS

Words and Music by
LEONARD SMITH

80

SANCTUARY

Words and Music by JOHN THOMPSON
and RANDY SCRUGGS

Moderately slow

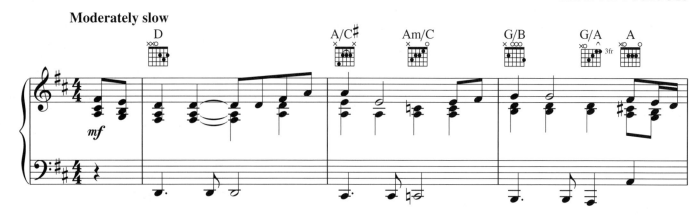

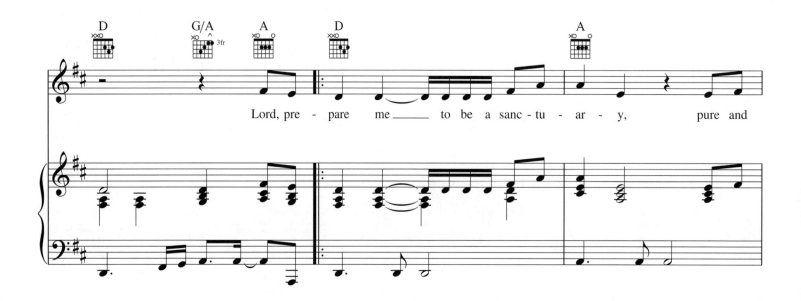

Lord, pre - pare me _____ to be a sanc-tu - ar - y, pure and

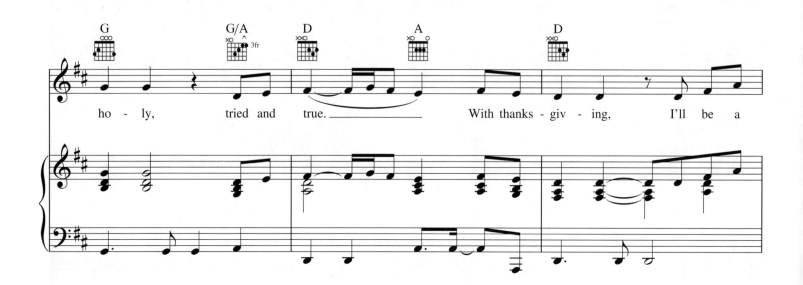

ho - ly, tried and true. _____ With thanks-giv - ing, I'll be a

SHINE, JESUS, SHINE

Words and Music by
GRAHAM KENDRICK

SPIRIT OF THE LIVING GOD

Words and Music by DANIEL IVERSON
and LOWELL ALEXANDER

Spir - it of the liv - ing God,
Soul of heav - en, heart of God,

fall fresh on me.
wash o - ver me. Spir - it of the
Soul of heav - en,

liv - ing God, fall fresh on me.
heart of God, wash o - ver me.

STEP BY STEP

Words and Music by
DAVID STRASSER "BEAKER"

O God, You are my __ God, and I will ev - er praise __ You. O God, You are my __ God, and I will ev - er praise __ You. I will seek You in the morn - ing, and I will learn to walk in Your __

THERE IS A REDEEMER

Words and Music by
MELODY GREEN

Moderately

1. There is a re- deem - er,
2.-4. *(See additional lyrics)*

Je - sus, God's own Son. _____

96

Additional Lyrics

2. Jesus, my redeemer,
   Name above all names.
   Precious Lamb of God, Messiah,
   Oh, for sinners slain. *(To Chorus)*

3. When I stand in glory,
   I will see His face,
   And there I'll serve my King forever
   In that holy place. *(To Chorus)*

4. There is a redeemer,
   Jesus, God's own Son.
   Precious Lamb of God, Messiah,
   Holy One. *(To Chorus)*

THOU ART WORTHY

Words and Music by
PAULINE MICHAEL MILLS

THERE IS NONE LIKE YOU

Words and Music by
LENNY LeBLANC

D.S. al Coda

THINK ABOUT HIS LOVE

Words and Music by
WALT HARRAH

THIS IS THE DAY

By LES GARRETT

THY WORD

Words and Music by MICHAEL W. SMITH
and AMY GRANT

WE BOW DOWN

Words and Music by
TWILA PARIS

You are _____

Lord of cre - a - tion and Lord of my _____ life,
King of cre - a - tion and King of my _____ life,

Lord of the land _____ and _____ the _____ sea. You were _____
King of the land _____ and _____ the _____ sea. You were _____

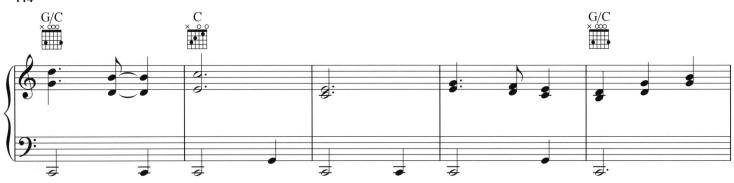

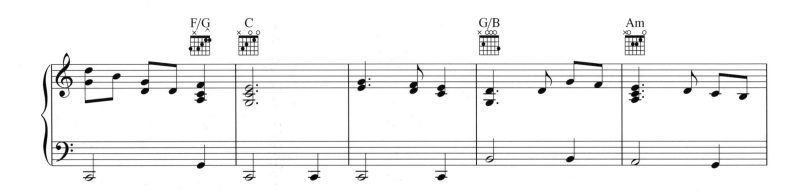

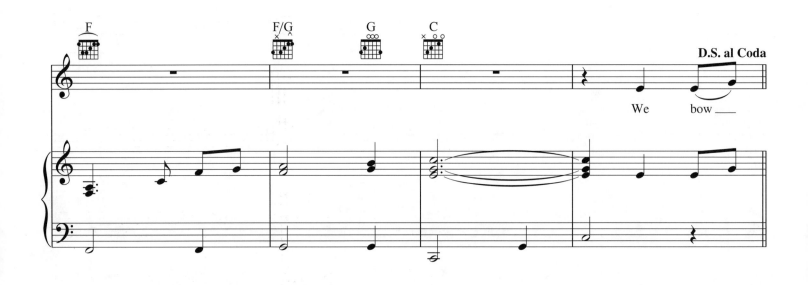

We bow ___

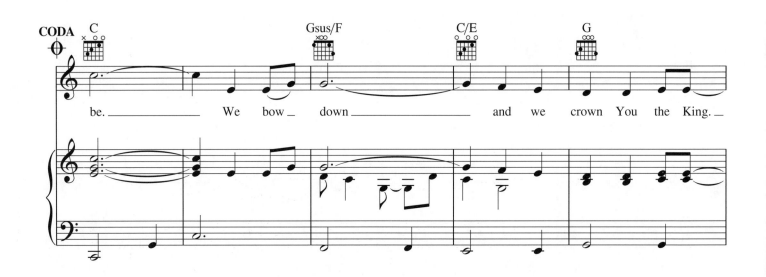

be. ___ We bow ___ down ___ and we crown You the King. ___

TO HIM WHO SITS ON THE THRONE

Words and Music by
DEBBYE C. GRAAFSMA

WORTHY THE LAMB
THAT WAS SLAIN

Words and Music by
DON MOEN

WORTHY, YOU ARE WORTHY

Words and Music by
DON MOEN

WE WILL GLORIFY

Words and Music by
TWILA PARIS

THE CHRISTIAN MUSICIAN

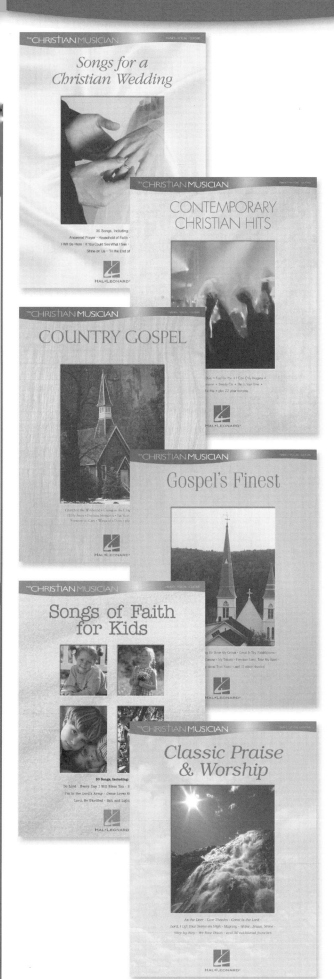

THE CHRISTIAN MUSICIAN series celebrates the many styles of music that make up the Christian faith. From Gospel favorites to today's hottest Christian artists, these books have something for all Christian musicians! There is no song duplication between any of the books!

CHRISTIAN ROCK

30 songs from today's hottest Contemporary Christian artists, including Audio Adrenaline, DC Talk, Delirious?, FFH, Jennifer Knapp, Jars of Clay, and Newsboys. Songs include: Consume Me • Everything • Flood • Get Down • Joy • One of These Days • Shine • Undo Me • and more.
00310953 Piano/Vocal/Guitar............$16.95

CLASSIC CONTEMPORARY CHRISTIAN

30 favorites essential to all Christian music repertoire, including: Arise, My Love • Awesome God • Friends • The Great Divide • His Strength Is Perfect • Love in Any Language • People Need the Lord • Where There Is Faith • and more.
00310954 Piano/Vocal/Guitar............$14.95

CLASSIC PRAISE & WORSHIP

Over 30 standards of the Praise & Worship movement, including: As the Deer • Great Is the Lord • He Is Exalted • Lord, I Lift Your Name on High • More Precious Than Silver • Oh Lord, You're Beautiful • Shine, Jesus, Shine • Step by Step • and more.
00310955 Piano/Vocal/Guitar............$14.95

CONTEMPORARY CHRISTIAN HITS

30 of today's top Christian favorites, from artists such as Avalon, Steven Curtis Chapman, DC Talk, MercyMe, Nichole Nordeman, Point of Grace, Rebecca St. James, ZOEgirl, and others. Songs include: Always Have, Always Will • Between You and Me • Can't Live a Day • Dive • Fool for You • God Is God • I Can Only Imagine • If This World • If You Want Me To • A Little More • Live Out Loud • My Will • Run to You • Steady On • Testify to Love • Wait for Me • and more.
00310952 Piano/Vocal/Guitar............$16.95

COUNTRY GOSPEL

Over 40 favorites, including: Church in the Wildwood • Crying in the Chapel • I Saw the Light • I Wouldn't Take Nothing for My Journey Now • Put Your Hand in the Hand • Turn Your Radio On • Will the Circle Be Unbroken • Wings of a Dove • and more.
00310961 Piano/Vocal/Guitar............$14.95

GOSPEL'S FINEST

Over 40 Gospel greats, including: Because He Lives • The Day He Wore My Crown • Great Is Thy Faithfulness • How Great Thou Art • In the Garden • More Than Wonderful • Precious Lord, Take My Hand • Soon and Very Soon • There's Something About That Name • and more.
00310959 Piano/Vocal/Guitar............$14.95

MODERN WORSHIP

Over 30 popular favorites of contemporary congregations, including: Above All • Ancient of Days • Breathe • The Heart of Worship • I Could Sing of Your Love Forever • It Is You • The Potter's Hand • Shout to the Lord • You Are My King (Amazing Love) • and more.
00310957 Piano/Vocal/Guitar............$14.95

SONGS FOR A CHRISTIAN WEDDING

35 songs suitable for services or receptions, including: Answered Prayer • Celebrate You • Doubly Good to You • Faithful Friend • Go There with You • Household of Faith • I Will Be Here • If You Could See What I See • My Place Is with You • Parent's Prayer (Let Go of Two) • Shine on Us • 'Til the End of Time • Where There Is Love • and more.
00310960 Piano/Vocal/Guitar............$16.95

SONGS OF FAITH FOR KIDS

50 favorites for kids of all ages! Includes: Arky, Arky • The B-I-B-L-E • Down in My Heart • God Is Bigger • He's Got the Whole World in His Hands • He's Still Workin' on Me • I'm in the Lord's Army • Lord, Be Glorified • Jesus Loves the Little Children • Salt and Light • This Little Light of Mine • Zacchaeus • and more.
00310958 Piano/Vocal/Guitar............$14.95

FOR MORE INFORMATION,
SEE YOUR LOCAL MUSIC DEALER,
OR WRITE TO:

HAL•LEONARD®
CORPORATION
7777 W. BLUEMOUND RD. P.O. BOX 13819
MILWAUKEE, WISCONSIN 53213

Visit Hal Leonard Online at
www.halleonard.com

Prices, contents, and availability subject to change without notice.

More Contemporary Christian Folios from Hal Leonard

AVALON – OXYGEN

Features all 11 songs from the 2001 release by this dynamic CCM vocal quartet: The Best Thing • By Heart, By Soul • Come and Fill My Heart • The Glory • I Don't Want to Go • Love Remains • Make It Last Forever • Oxygen • Never Givin' Up • Undeniably You • Wonder Why.

_____00306440 Piano/Vocal/Guitar $14.95

STEVEN CURTIS CHAPMAN – DECLARATION

13 songs: Bring It On • Carry You to Jesus • Declaration of Dependence • God Follower • God Is God • Jesus Is Life • Live Out Loud • Magnificent Obsession • No Greater Love • Savior • See the Glory • This Day • When Love Takes You In.

_____00306453 Piano/Vocal/Guitar $14.95

DC TALK – INTERMISSION: THE GREATEST HITS

17 of DC Talk's best: Between You and Me • Chance • Colored People • Consume Me • Hardway (Remix) • I Wish We'd All Been Ready • In the Light • Jesus Freak • Jesus Is Just Alright • Luv Is a Verb • Mind's Eye • My Will • Say the Words (Now) • Socially Acceptable • SugarCoat It • Supernatural • What If I Stumble.

_____00306414 Piano/Vocal/Guitar $14.95

DELIRIOUS? – GLO

All the songs from the brand new release by these British Christian rockers. Includes: Awaken the Dawn • Everything • God You Are My God • God's Romance • Hang On to You • Intimate Stranger • Investigate • Jesus' Blood • My Glorious • What Would I Have Done? • The Years Go By.

_____00306386 Piano/Vocal/Guitar $14.95

JEFF DEYO – SATURATE

Features 14 powerful tracks, including: All I Want • I Give You My Heart • I'd Rather Have Jesus • Let It Flow • Let Me Burn • Lose Myself • Many Crowns • More Love, More Power • Satisfy • Sing to You • Thank You for Life • You Are Good • You Are Good (Piano & Cello Movement) • You Are Good (Orchestral Movement).

_____00306484 Piano/Vocal/Guitar $14.95

THE KATINAS – LIFESTYLE

Features 14 songs, including their hit "Thank You" and: Beauty of Your Grace • Breathe • Chant • Draw Me Close • Eagle's Wings • I Give You My Heart • I Love You Lord • Live Your Love • Lord, I Lift Your Name on High • Mighty River • Rejoice • Trading My Sorrows • You Are Good.

_____00306485 Piano/Vocal/Guitar $14.95

JENNIFER KNAPP – THE WAY I AM

Includes all 12 tunes from the critically acclaimed CD: Around Me • Breathe on Me • By and By • Charity • Come to Me • Fall Down • In Two (The Lament) • Light of the World • No Regrets • Say Won't You Say • Sing Mary Sing • The Way I Am.

_____00306467 Piano/Vocal/Guitar $14.95

THE MARTINS – GLORIFY/EDIFY/TESTIFY

Features 16 songs: Be Thou My Vision • Gentle Shepherd • Healer of My Heart • In Christ Alone • Jesus, I Am Resting • Lord Most High • Pass Me Not • Redeemed • Settle on My Soul • So High • You Are Holy • more. Includes vocal harmony parts.

_____00306492 Piano/Vocal/Guitar $14.95

BABBIE MASON – NO BETTER PLACE

10 songs from this gospel diva: Change Me Now • Holy Spirit, You Are Welcome Here • The House That Love Built • I Will Be the One • Isn't That Just Like God • Love to the Highest Power • Only God Can Heal • Pray On • Show Some Sign • Stay Up on the Wall.

_____00306357 Piano/Vocal/Guitar $14.95

NICHOLE NORDEMAN – WOVEN & SPUN

Includes all 11 songs from the 2002 release of this Dove Award nominee: Doxology • Even Then • Gratitude • Healed • Holy • I Am • Legacy • Mercies New • My Offering • Never Loved You More • Take Me As I Am.

_____00306494 Piano/Vocal/Guitar $14.95

STACIE ORRICO – GENUINE

This debut release from Orrico features 13 songs: Confidant • Dear Friend • Don't Look at Me • Everything • Genuine • Holdin' On • O.O Baby • Restore My Soul • Ride • So Pray • Stay True • With a Little Faith • Without Love.

_____00306417 Piano/Vocal/Guitar $14.95

THE BEST OF OUT OF EDEN

A great compilation of 13 hit songs: Come and Take My Hand • A Friend • Get to Heaven • Greater Love • If You Really Knew Me • Lookin' for Love • More Than You Know • River • Show Me • There Is a Love • and more.

_____00306381 Piano/Vocal/Guitar $14.95

TWILA PARIS – GREATEST HITS

This folio celebrates Twila's career with 18 hits: Destiny • Faithful Friend • God Is in Control • He Is Exalted • How Beautiful • Lamb of God • Run to You • The Time Is Now • We Bow Down • We Will Glorify • and more.

_____00306449 Piano/Vocal/Guitar $14.95

PHILLIPS, CRAIG AND DEAN – LET MY WORDS BE FEW

This 10-song collection includes: Come, Now Is the Time to Worship • How Great You Are • Let Everything That Has Breath • Let My Words Be Few • Open the Eyes of My Heart • You Are My King • Your Grace Still Amazes Me • and more.

_____00306437 Piano/Vocal/Guitar $14.95

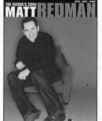

MATT REDMAN – THE FATHER'S SONG

Features 14 songs: The Father's Song • Holy Moment • Justice and Mercy • King of This Heart • Let My Words Be Few • Light of the World • Nothing Is Too Much • O Sacred King • Revelation • Take the World but Give Me Jesus • You Must Increase • more.

_____00306378 Piano/Vocal/Guitar $14.95

REBECCA ST. JAMES – WORSHIP GOD

Includes 12 worship tunes: Above All • Better Is One Day • Breathe • God of Wonders • It Is Well with My Soul • Lamb of God • Let My Words Be Few • More Than the Watchmen • Omega (Remix) • Quiet You with My Love • Song of Love • You.

_____00306473 Piano/Vocal/Guitar $14.95

ZOEGIRL

11 terrific songs from this debut album: Anything Is Possible • Constantly • Give Me One Reason • I Believe • Little Did I Know • Live Life • Living for You • No You • Stop Right There • Suddenly • Upside Down.

_____00306455 Piano/Vocal/Guitar $14.95

FOR MORE INFORMATION, SEE YOUR LOCAL MUSIC DEALER, OR WRITE TO:

HAL•LEONARD® CORPORATION

7777 W. BLUEMOUND RD. P.O. BOX 13819 MILWAUKEE, WI 53213

For a complete listing of the products we have available, Visit Hal Leonard online at
www.halleonard.com

Prices, contents and availability subject to change without notice.

0203